To Josh Griffey

PISCES

A guide to living your best astrological life

STELLA ANDROMEDA

ILLUSTRATED BY EVI O. STUDIO

Hardie Grant

BOOKS

Introduction 7

I.

Get to Know Pisces

Pisces characteristics	31
Physical Pisces	34
How Pisces communicates	37
Pisces careers	38
How Pisces chimes	41
Who loves whom?	44

II.

The Pisces Deep Dive

The Pisces home	55
Self-care	57
Food and cooking	59
How Pisces handles money	61
How Pisces handles the boss	62
What is Pisces like to live with?	65
How to handle a break-up	66
How Pisces wants to be loved	69
Pisces' sex life	72

III.

Give Me More

Your birth chart   76
The Moon effect   80
The 10 planets   83
The four elements   89
Cardinal, fixed and mutable signs   92
The 12 houses   95
The ascendant   101
Saturn return   103
Mercury retrograde   104

Further reading   108
Acknowledgements   109
About the author   111

Introduction

Inscribed on the forecourt of the ancient Greek temple of Apollo at Delphi are the words 'know thyself'. This is one of the 147 Delphic maxims, or rules to live by, attributed to Apollo himself, and was later extended by the philosopher Socrates to the sentence, 'The unexamined life is not worth living.'

People seek a variety of ways of knowing themselves, of coming to terms with life and trying to find ways to understand the challenges of human existence, often through therapy or belief systems like organised religion. These are ways in which we strive to understand the relationships we have with ourselves and others better, seeking out particular tools that enable us to do so.

As far as systems of understanding human nature and experience go, astrology has much to offer through its symbolic use of the constellations of the heavens, the depictions of the zodiac signs, the planets and their energetic effects. Many people find accessing this information and harnessing its potential a useful way of thinking about how to manage their lives more effectively.

What is astrology?

In simple terms, astrology is the study and interpretation of how the planets can influence us, and the world in which we live, through an understanding of their positions at a specific place in time. The practice of astrology relies on a combination of factual knowledge of the characteristics of these positions and their psychological interpretation.

Astrology is less of a belief system and more of a tool for living, from which ancient and established wisdom can be drawn. Any of us can learn to use astrology, not so much for divination or telling the future, but as a guidebook that provides greater insight and a more thoughtful way of approaching life. Timing is very much at the heart of astrology, and knowledge of planetary configurations and their relationship to each other at specific moments in time can assist in helping us with the timing of some of our life choices and decisions.

Knowing when major life shifts can occur – because of particular planetary configurations such as a Saturn return (see page 103) or Mercury retrograde (see page 104) – or what it means to have Venus in your seventh house (see pages 85 and 98), while recognising the specific characteristics of your sign, are all tools that you can use to your advantage. Knowledge is power, and astrology can be a very powerful supplement to approaching life's ups and downs and any relationships we form along the way.

The 12 signs of the zodiac

Each sign of the zodiac has a range of recognisable characteristics, shared by people born under that sign. This is your Sun sign, which you probably already know – and the usual starting point from which we each begin to explore our own astrological paths. Sun sign characteristics can be strongly exhibited in an individual's make-up; however, this is only part of the picture.

Usually, how we appear to others is tempered by the influence of other factors – and these are worth bearing in mind. Your ascendant sign is equally important, as is the positioning of your Moon. You can also look to your opposite sign to see what your Sun sign may need a little more of, to balance its characteristics.

After getting to know your Sun sign in the first part of this book, you might want to dive into the Give Me More section (see pages 74–105) to start to explore all the particulars of your birth chart. These will give you far greater insight into the myriad astrological influences that may play out in your life.

Sun signs

It takes 365 (and a quarter, to be precise) days for the Earth to orbit the Sun and in so doing, the Sun appears to us to spend a month travelling through each sign of the zodiac. Your Sun sign is therefore an indication of the sign that the Sun was travelling through at the time of your birth. Knowing what Sun signs you and your family, friends and lovers are provides you with just the beginning of the insights into character and personality that astrology can help you discover.

On the cusp

For those for whom a birthday falls close to the end of one Sun sign and the beginning of another, it's worth knowing what time you were born. There's no such thing, astrologically, as being 'on the cusp' – because the signs begin at a specific time on a specific date, although this can vary a little year on year. If you are not sure, you'll need to know your birth date, birth time and birth place to work out accurately to which Sun sign you belong. Once you have these, you can consult an astrologer or run your details through an online astrology site program (see page 108) to give you the most accurate birth chart possible.

Taurus

The bull

21 APRIL–20 MAY

Grounded, sensual and appreciative of bodily pleasures, Taurus is a fixed earth sign endowed by its ruling planet Venus with grace and a love of beauty, despite its depiction as a bull. Generally characterised by an easy and uncomplicated, if occasionally stubborn, approach to life, Taurus' opposite sign is watery Scorpio.

Aries

The ram

21 MARCH–20 APRIL

Astrologically the first sign of the zodiac, Aries appears alongside the vernal (or spring) equinox. A cardinal fire sign, depicted by the ram, it is the sign of beginnings and ruled by planet Mars, which represents a dynamic ability to meet challenges energetically and creatively. Its opposite sign is airy Libra.

Gemini

The twins

✴

21 MAY-20 JUNE

A mutable air sign symbolised by
the twins, Gemini tends to see both
sides of an argument, its speedy
intellect influenced by its ruling
planet Mercury. Tending to fight
shy of commitment, this sign also
epitomises a certain youthfulness
of attitude. Its opposite sign is
fiery Sagittarius.

Cancer

The crab

✴

21 JUNE-21 JULY

Depicted by the crab and the
tenacity of its claws, Cancer is a
cardinal water sign, emotional and
intuitive, its sensitivity protected
by its shell. Ruled by the maternal
Moon, the shell also represents the
security of home, to which Cancer
is committed. Its opposite sign is
earthy Capricorn.

Leo

The lion

22 JULY–21 AUGUST

A fixed fire sign, ruled by the Sun, Leo loves to shine and is an idealist at heart, positive and generous to a fault. Depicted by the lion, Leo can roar with pride and be confident and uncompromising, with a great faith and trust in humanity. Its opposite sign is airy Aquarius.

Virgo

The virgin

22 AUGUST–21 SEPTEMBER

Traditionally represented as a maiden or virgin, this mutable earth sign is observant, detail oriented and tends towards self-sufficiency. Ruled by Mercury, Virgo benefits from a sharp intellect that can be self-critical, while often being very health conscious. Its opposite sign is watery Pisces.

Scorpio

The scorpion

✴

22 OCTOBER–21 NOVEMBER

Given to intense feelings, as
befits a fixed water sign, Scorpio
is depicted by the scorpion – linking
it to the rebirth that follows death –
and is ruled by both Pluto and Mars.
With a strong spirituality and deep
emotions, Scorpio needs security to
transform its strength. Its opposite
sign is earthy Taurus.

Libra

The scales

✴

22 SEPTEMBER–21 OCTOBER

A cardinal air sign, ruled by Venus,
Libra is all about beauty, balance
(as depicted by the scales) and
harmony in its rather romanticised,
ideal world. With a strong aesthetic
sense, Libra can be both arty and
crafty, but also likes fairness and
can be very diplomatic. Its
opposite sign is fiery Aries.

Sagittarius

The archer

✴

22 NOVEMBER–21 DECEMBER

Depicted by the archer, Sagittarius is a mutable fire sign that's all about travel and adventure, in body or mind, and is very direct in approach. Ruled by the benevolent Jupiter, Sagittarius is optimistic with lots of ideas; liking a free rein, but with a tendency to generalise. Its opposite sign is airy Gemini.

Capricorn

The goat

✴

22 DECEMBER–20 JANUARY

Ruled by Saturn, Capricorn is a cardinal earth sign associated with hard work and depicted by the sure-footed and sometimes playful goat. Trustworthy and unafraid of commitment, Capricorn is often very self-sufficient and has the discipline for the freelance working life. Its opposite sign is the watery Cancer.

Aquarius
The water carrier

★

21 JANUARY–19 FEBRUARY

Confusingly, given its depiction by the water carrier, Aquarius is a fixed air sign ruled by the unpredictable Uranus, sweeping away old ideas with innovative thinking. Tolerant, open-minded and all about humanity, its vision is social with a conscience. Its opposite sign is fiery Leo.

Pisces
The fish

20 FEBRUARY–20 MARCH

Acutely responsive to its surroundings, Pisces is a mutable water sign depicted by two fish, swimming in opposite directions, sometimes confusing fantasy with reality. Ruled by Neptune, its world is fluid, imaginative and empathetic, often picking up on the moods of others. Its opposite sign is earthy Virgo.

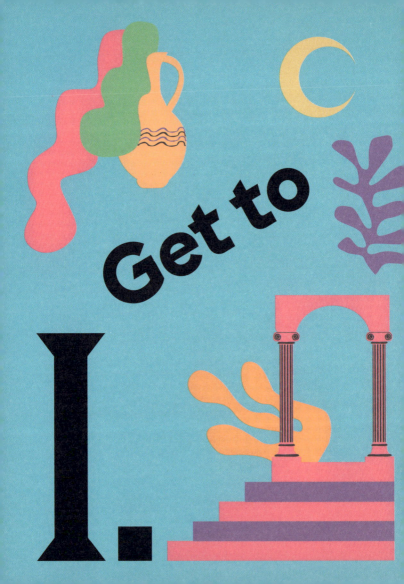

Get to

I.

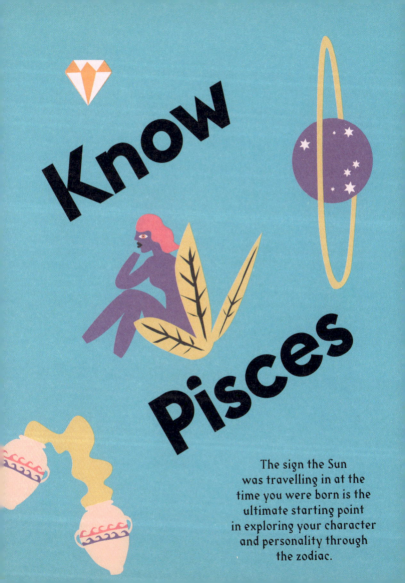

Know
Pisces

The sign the Sun
was travelling in at the
time you were born is the
ultimate starting point
in exploring your character
and personality through
the zodiac.

Mutable water sign, depicted by two fish, joined but swimming in opposite directions.

Ruled by Neptune, a planet that is all about fantasy, mystery and possible deception.

OPPOSITE SIGN

Virgo

STATEMENT OF SELF

'I believe.'

Lucky colour

As might be expected, the turquoise blue-greens
of the ever-changing light and dark of the sea are
Pisces' lucky colours. Wear these colours when you need
a psychological boost and additional courage. If you
don't want to commit head-to-toe, choose blue or green
for accessories – shoes, gloves, socks or even underwear.

Lucky day

Friday. The last day of the working week (for most of us) connects to the twelfth and last sign of the Zodiac. Friday also links to the Old English goddess, Frigg, who was (in Norse terms) *a völva,* a female practitioner of magic, a spiritual leader and healer.

Lucky gem

Aquamarine, with its name derived from the Latin for seawater, is Pisces' lucky stone. It is calming and cleansing to the mind, said to promote serenity and healing and a protective talisman for sailors and seafarers.

Locations

Countries that energise and resonate with the Pisces soul are Portugal, Morocco, Samoa and Egypt; while cities like Seville, Dublin, Warsaw, Bournemouth and Jerusalem all chime with a sense of Piscean karma.

V.

Holidays

Inevitably, water-based holidays will appeal, whether this is sailing the Norfolk broads on an old canal boat, riding the rapids or fishing along the Nile on a felucca. Failing that, scuba diving in the Maldives wil always work. For Pisces to relax and regenerate, it's all about the water (and the fish), and maybe a glamorous spa thrown in for good measure.

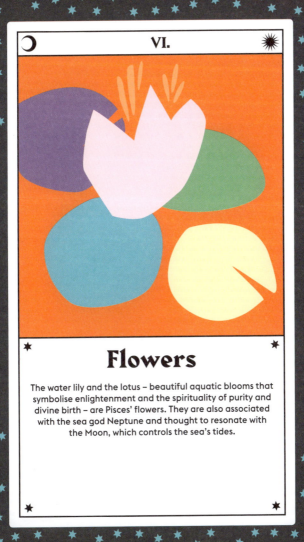

Flowers

The water lily and the lotus – beautiful aquatic blooms that symbolise enlightenment and the spirituality of purity and divine birth – are Pisces' flowers. They are also associated with the sea god Neptune and thought to resonate with the Moon, which controls the sea's tides.

Trees

The willow tree, and the weeping willow in particular, with its affinity for water, is Pisces' tree, its graceful leaves reaching into the water and creating a mysterious shroud over it. The willow is also associated with healing qualities – willow bark contains salicin, which the body converts to salicylic acid, a precursor of anti-inflammatory and pain-relieving aspirin.

VIII.

Pets

A beguiling tank full of beautiful tropical fish will bring great pleasure to Pisces, who will also find that spending time watching them both soothes the soul and stimulates the imagination. Even a couple of goldfish in a bowl appeals.

IX.

Parties

Pisces is a generous and gregarious soul who loves to throw a party, often spontaneously as they are not meticulous planners. There's a glamorous and artistic side to Pisces, too, so expect some imaginative ideas when it comes to classy drinks. A Blueberry Champagne Shrub might feature, or something with blue Curaçao liqueur as its base.

Pisces
characteristics

Imaginative, empathic, intuitive and sometimes spiritual to the point of being mystical, Pisces has a quicksilver mind, like fish catching the light as they dart through the watery depths in which they thrive. This twelfth astrological sign of the zodiac is all about the deep spiritual regeneration that heralds spring (as embodied in the sign that follows, Aries). And as a water sign, Pisces links the two worlds of internal and external life, existing at a point on the cusp of reality and in the realms of imagination, making them one of the most naturally creative of the signs.

That Pisces lives comfortably with their emotions goes without saying. They literally feel their way through life and when they say, 'I know how you feel', they do and are being empathetic to the nth degree. This is what makes Pisces so intuitive: they just can't help feeling what you're feeling.

This makes Pisces amongst the most attentive of friends, very capable of putting others' needs before their own – sometimes to their own detriment, as feeling everything so strongly can become overwhelming. In order to survive, Pisces has to learn to manage these strong emotions, ensuring that they don't lose sight of themselves. These qualities also make it easy for Pisces to read a social situation and adapt accordingly; and to read people well, too, making them amongst the most successful of poker players!

Pisces creativity is legendary and comes from an ability to almost literally lose themselves in the realms of their imagination. Once harnessed, this imagination is not only creative in an artistic sense, but also in a practical way and they are consequently one of the most able of problem-solvers. That's what can be so unexpected about these dreamy souls: they can also really graft and deliver as long as they are fully involved in something they really care about. Pisces does need to control their urge just to be swept along on the current of their ideas, though, and to make sure they don't lose sight of what's actually possible. If they can do this, their big dreams are often successfully realised.

Their kindness and quicksilver mind make Pisces witty and attractive company and they are seldom short of friends, although they are quite discerning about those with whom they wish to spend their time, valuing authenticity and ideas in others over superficial relationships.

SOFTENING THE WATER

The key characteristics of any Sun sign can be balanced out (or sometimes reinforced) by the characteristics of other signs in the same birth chart, particularly those of the ascendant and the Moon. So if someone doesn't appear to be typical of their Sun sign, that's why. However, those nascent Pisces aspects will always be there as a key influence, informing an individual's approach to life.

Physical Pisces

Often very lithe on their feet with quick, graceful movements, Pisces seems to swim easily both with and against the tide, adapting their position as they weave their way through life. Overall, however, they are not the most physically robust of signs, they lack raw energy and they can be prone to water retention and vulnerable to weepy sinuses and colds. Their emotional health can also fluctuate as they are so sensitive to the currents of feeling around them, picking up on other people's vibes and getting caught up in them, that it can overwhelm them. It's as well then for Pisces to surround themselves with upbeat people who can inspire them and promote a more realistic and secure attitude.

Health

The feet, the soles of the body, are ruled by Pisces and it's here that problems might arise, particularly if their artistic nature leads them into the world of dance. In others, athlete's foot, gout, corns and bunions might be a problem. Pisces' emotional health can also be an issue, where mental over-stimulation, over-thinking and over-tiredness can all lead to worry and exhaustion. There's also a tendency amongst some Pisces to self-medicate against this with alcohol and other drugs, in an attempt to relieve symptoms of emotional stress – because of this, Pisces is the sign most likely to have a problem with addiction.

Exercise

Although swimming is an excellent way for Pisces to immerse themselves in a physical exercise that also relieves stress, it's also important for them to 'ground' themselves through their feet, so walking and running are good, too. Relieving tension in the body also helps relieve the tension in the mind, especially if exercise is used as a form of meditation and 'time out'.

How Pisces communicates

Pisces is a good and thoughtful listener who often responds not only with empathy but also with creative ideas and suggestions for how to approach a problem or situation. They are good for talking things through, as long as they can keep on point – and here may lie a small problem, as Pisces can meander off into long and sometimes complicated thought processes. It may not always be easy to see where they are leading, but if you go with their flow, Pisces usually gets there in the end even if it may feel at times as if you are, literally, swimming upstream or against the tide.

Pisces' narrative style can make their communication rather long winded. This makes them one of the great storytellers of the zodiac and, although truthful in essence, they may embroider reality a little for good effect. Not letting the facts stand in the way of a good story may be entertaining, but Pisces should be aware that accuracy is sometimes a more helpful approach.

Pisces
careers

Often inspired and inspiring, adaptable Pisces can lend their skills to a variety of careers that involve people, creativity and the world of ideas –in everything from art to business. Any problem-solving activity is right up there, too, while their ability to read people makes them good at management and promoting harmony in the workplace.

Working as a therapist might also interest empathic Pisces, or in an allied profession like industrial psychology, counselling or career coaching. If spiritual, this might extend into the realms of religion and spiritual advisor, as a vicar, monk, imam or rabbi. And then there are those more literal water-based careers that might be of interest – from fisherman to sailor or marine biologist – for those fascinated by the sea's watery depths.

What should not be underestimated, though, is how successful Pisces can be in the world of business. Creativity, vision and their ability to problem solve and read people are a potent mix, which might explain why they are often so successful and make a great deal of money.

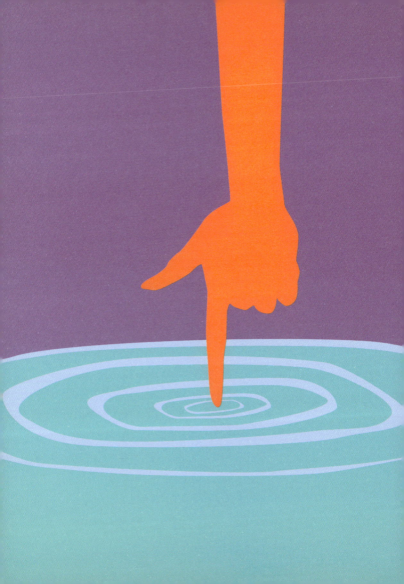

How Pisces chimes

From lovers to friends, when it comes to other signs, how does Pisces get along? Knowledge of other signs and the ways in which they interact can be helpful when negotiating relationships, revealed through an understanding of Sun sign characteristics that might chime or chafe. Understanding these through an astrological framework can be really helpful as it can depersonalise potential frictions, taking the sting out of what appears to be in opposition.

Harmonising relationships can sometimes appear to be a problem to ponder rather than an opportunity to explore, but how Pisces chimes with other signs is partly dependent on what other planetary influences are at play in their personal birth chart, toning down or enhancing aspects of their Sun sign characteristics, especially those that can sometimes clash with other signs.

The Pisces woman

There's a dreamy, romantic look to the Pisces woman that says love is extremely important. Don't mistake her for being a pushover, however, as she is generally shrewd enough to know the real thing when she sees it, and when it comes to finding her dream partner, she can be surprisingly realistic as a result.

NOTABLE PISCES WOMEN

Where would we be without the vision of Associate Justice of the US Supreme Court Ruth Bader Ginsburg? There's a self-possession about the most successful of Pisces women, including super-feminine actress Elizabeth Taylor, Barbadian singer, producer and business woman Rihanna and actress, producer and LGBT activist Ellen Page.

The Pisces man

Attentive, sensitive and witty, the Pisces man is a recognisable charmer because he has an appreciation of people, he likes getting to know them and he applies his emotional imagination to promote romance in almost any situation. He is generally a giver and not a taker, but this can be a way of keeping other people's excessive emotion at bay.

Who could be a more successful Pisces than visionary Steve Jobs, co-founder of Apple? He is up there with theoretical physicist Albert Einstein and Renaissance painter, poet, sculptor and architect Michelangelo. Brooding Bond actor Daniel Craig and pioneering film director Spike Lee are both Pisces, too.

Who love

whom?

Pisces & Aries

Unlikely as it might initially seem, there's a complementary link between Pisces' dreamy nature and need for security and Aries' more dynamic and assured approach to life that can work quite well between these two, as long as some tact is applied.

Pisces & Taurus

Taurus' extreme practicality is wonderfully useful in helping to realise the scope of Pisces' vision, but can sometimes be a little too heavy-handed for such a romantic, even though their mutual taste for creature comforts is well shared.

Pisces & Gemini

Both quick-witted by nature, there's an immediate attraction but one that is unlikely to be sustained given Pisces' dislike of Gemini's airy thoughtlessness, while Gemini tends to find Pisces' intense need for emotional reassurance impossible to fathom.

Pisces & Cancer

Both equally emotional and sensitive, Cancer has the edge on practicality which helps balance this pairing and keep what could be rather a too-fluid relationship, stable. Once committed they are loyal to each other, although it might take them a while to settle.

Pisces & Leo

Tricky this one: Leo can't understand Pisces' dreamy hesitancy and tends to stomp all over their finer feelings. In turn, Pisces doesn't understand Leo's need for acknowledgement and admiration and also hates the lion's endless need to socialise.

Pisces & Virgo

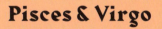

Astrological opposites can complement each other well, but Virgo's extremely fastidious mind can find Pisces' inclination to prioritise dreams over reality completely maddening. There's unlikely to be enough romance, either, between these two.

Pisces & Scorpio

There's an immediate closeness between these two potentially intense water signs, where Scorpio's possessiveness actually helps Pisces feel loved rather than smothered, and they are equally sensual and imaginative with a strong sexual bond.

Pisces & Libra

There can be an initial harmony between these two, because both like the artistic side of life and share a similar vision of what's beautiful, but Pisces' need for emotional security is at odds with Libra's desire for freedom, and this might undermine them in the end.

Pisces & Sagittarius

The possible flaw here is Sagittarius' need for independence and constant activity outside the home, which Pisces finds very undermining. There's a restlessness that feels like rejection to Pisces, while Pisces' dreamy romanticism irritates Sagittarius in turn.

Pisces & Aquarius

Innovative Aquarius seems a perfect match for Pisces' sensual idealism but there's too much airy detachment in their ideas to fully engage with Pisces' emotional approach. Plus, Aquarius needs external stimulation, which frustrates Pisces' need for intimacy.

Pisces & Pisces

There's probably too much sharing of a good thing here – sensitivity, romance, empathy, dreams and ideas – to make this relationship work well in real life. All this emotional fluidity could overwhelm them both, leading to an unhelpful interdependence.

Pisces & Capricorn

An example of opposites attracting and complementing each other, these two are really well matched because Pisces relishes Capricorn's passion, strength of character and can-do attitude, while Capricorn loves Pisces' affectionate nature and romanticism.

Pisces love-o-meter

Least compatible

Leo Virgo Aquarius Sagittarius Pisces Gemini

Most compatible

Libra Taurus Aries Cancer Capricorn Scorpio

The Pisces

II.

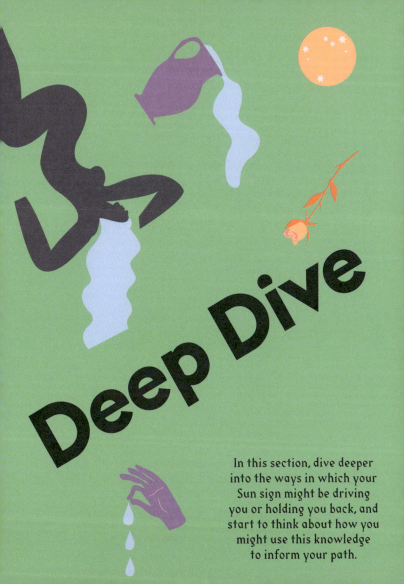

Deep Dive

In this section, dive deeper into the ways in which your Sun sign might be driving you or holding you back, and start to think about how you might use this knowledge to inform your path.

The
Pisces
home

A water feature may well be at the heart of a home belonging to Pisces, whether this is a large aquarium full of tropical fish or a small bowl with two goldfish. There may even be a pond in the garden. Failing that, seascapes or fish-related artwork may hang on the walls, or other references to shells and aquamarine life may be visible in their chosen home décor, including the use of blue, blue-green or turquoise colour schemes. There may also be a sensual, tactile nature to furnishing fabrics, silky fabrics or those with a satin sheen, reminiscent of the gleaming, light-catching aspect of water.

There's also likely to be evidence of their more artistic side. This can range from a work room or studio to a small corner filled with artist's materials. Or there may be shelves of art books, feeding Pisces' creative soul. The Pisces home is often full of visitors and conversation, too, as there is a social, gregarious, welcoming side to this caring sign.

TOP TIPS FOR
PISCES' SELF-CARE

★ Reflexology, a foot massage
  or a pedicure will all help
  ground Pisces.

★ Strengthening their core
  muscles can help Pisces feel
  more stable.

★ Keep well hydrated to help
  those over-active brain cells
  stay happy.

Self-care

When it comes to looking after themselves, Pisces needs to work towards grounding all their fluctuating thoughts in the real world, balancing the mind with the body so that they exist together as a harmonious whole. It's all too easy for Pisces to get lost in their head and spend long hours working away at their desk only to then wonder why they feel a little out of touch with their surroundings. To balance this, anything that can be done physically to reconnect, or to ground feelings in some sort of real-world experience, is all to the good.

Regular meals are a good start and also a way to socialise with a communal focus, which Pisces always enjoys. Regular exercise (swimming comes as a natural choice) is really important as is the inclusion of some way to reconnect and ground their body and mind. T'ai Chi is good, and yoga can incorporate a more spiritual side to exercise, especially something like a Vinyasa flow practice. Pilates helps root the physical experience very much in the body through its core, which can really help balance the more cerebral side of Pisces.

WHAT TO KEEP IN THE PISCES PANTRY

* Tinned (canned) sardines for an instant protein hit.

* Gourmet sea salt flakes for seasoning.

* Dried figs to add a little natural sweetness to their diet.

Food
and
cooking

Unsurprisingly, there's a tendency for Pisces to turn cooking into something of an art form. Certainly, they'll want their food to look wonderful and they may become adept at creating a stylish plate of delicious ingredients, sometimes giving greater priority to what it looks like (and how to style it for Instagram) than to its taste.

In terms of diet, seafood of all sorts may be a Pisces favourite, but they're also a sign that can take a rather spiritual approach to their diet, embracing something like veganism or, at the least, vegetarianism in support of their fellow creatures on earth. Pisces is unlikely to be a faddy eater – and even if they favour a specific dietary regime, they won't try to impose their choice on others.

TOP TIPS FOR PISCES' MONEY

* Be more proactive about saving for a rainy day.

* Always double check financial advice as being canny about money isn't always Pisces' strong suit.

* If there's a secret stash anywhere, Pisces needs to ensure it's legal.

How Pisces handles money

Pisces isn't that bothered about accumulating vast sums of money for the sake of it: it's not really up there with their spiritual values. But they do recognise that having money makes life easier, allowing it to flow along smoothly. For that reason, Pisces will generally work hard towards ensuring they have enough. Plus, because they have such vision and read people so well, somehow making money comes quite easily to them. Keeping it may be another issue for Pisces, because investing in dreams isn't as secure as investing in bricks and mortar, although Pisces does have great faith, and with good reason, in their own creativity and ability.

Pisces is by nature a generous soul and although they are not an easy touch, they are likely to share their hard-earned cash with those in need, with little thought to their own future. Smart Pisces knows, too, they have to get the balance of incoming and outgoing money right and that includes saving for a rainy day.

How Pisces handles the boss

Pisces' thoughtfulness means that they are usually more than considerate of the needs of their work colleagues and this makes them a natural team player. They can be quite inspirational to others, while their natural enthusiasm and willingness to graft makes them popular. Pisces looks towards the greater good of an organisation and they aren't possessive about their accomplishments, all of which finds favour with their boss. That's Pisces' other secret skill: they are often very good people managers, and this includes handling their boss well, too.

Generally, Pisces are such personable people that they are easy to employ and get along with. They know their own value and the value of what they contribute. When – and if – Pisces has a problem, they can usually sweet talk their way out of trouble, trusting in the fact that having successfully delivered in the past, this will stand them in good stead. On this basis, they can even throw a sickie, occasionally, without damaging their reputation.

TOP TIPS TO HANDLE THE BOSS

★ Don't exploit Pisces' reputation for schmoozing: use it only when necessary.

★ Deliver on those creative ideas, don't dump that part of the job on others.

★ Utilise opportunities that expand experience to build career prospects.

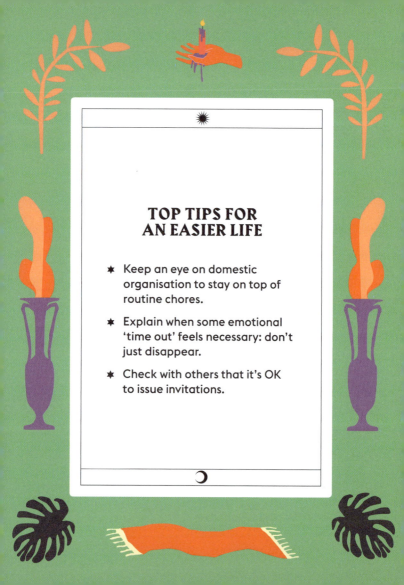

TOP TIPS FOR
AN EASIER LIFE

★ Keep an eye on domestic organisation to stay on top of routine chores.

★ Explain when some emotional 'time out' feels necessary: don't just disappear.

★ Check with others that it's OK to issue invitations.

What is Pisces like to live with?

Pisces can make a captivating partner or housemate because their natural affection, playfulness and sensitivity makes them very attuned to those around them. This makes them amongst the most thoughtful of people to live with, *except* when they disappear into a world of their own. Then, practical considerations of domesticity in particular can take a back seat while Pisces is preoccupied with whatever project or idea (or obsession) is currently occupying their imagination and creative mind. But Pisces are responsive people, too, so it only takes a little nudge to remind them of their responsibility to those they live with and, once reminded, they will gladly drop everything to do their bit.

It's a rare Pisces that chooses to live completely alone; they are not the hermits of the zodiac and prefer company. Pisces like to host visitors, too, to whom they offer anything from a meal to a bed for the night to an extended visit – sometimes without checking with partners or housemates first.

How to handle a break-up

There's a very private, not to say secretive side, to Pisces who can become extremely elusive when hurt, retiring to deep contemplation of a failed relationship or of their ex, regardless of who has done the breaking-up. Pisces is usually hopeless about asking for emotional support or help at this time, but needs to be realistic and not carry a torch for a lost love. Pisces hates hurting others and feels things so keenly that they have a tendency to feel the other person's pain almost as much as their own. This can become overwhelming, causing them to react by withdrawing from society, or into other forms of escapism, taking a while to recover. In this way, there's a tendency for Pisces to indulge their sorrow rather than confronting it and taking more positive steps to manage it.

TOP TIPS FOR
AN EASIER BREAK-UP

★ Be kind to yourself and confide in a close friend to help you move on.

★ A routine of *sleep, eat, work, exercise, rest, repeat* will help you get through the first few weeks until feelings resolve.

★ Avoid hiding from reality and address issues as they come up.

How Pisces wants to be loved

Affectionate, romantic and sometimes a tad mystical when it comes to loving, inevitably this is also pretty much how Pisces wants to be loved in return, too. Think of that knight in shining armour on a gleaming white horse, or the princess in the tower: probably both Pisces. It's all about the imaginative playing out of the wooing and being wooed, where it is written in the stars. But Pisces doesn't make it easy for themselves. This is the sign most likely to believe in love at first sight, soul mates and the sheer transcendence of spiritual union. All of which can be brought down to earth with a bit of a bump as reality bites and that unicorn disappears off into the sunset. No matter, Pisces can generate love enough for two and is soon off on another romantic quest.

Often Pisces also needs to feel needed, which can create a tendency to gravitate towards emotionally needy people, who may not be capable of loving Pisces quite enough in return.

If this happens, there's often an imbalance, which can be problematic. It's important not to be blinded by the mere look of love and for Pisces to keep one foot on the floor until they know for sure.

Pisces also needs to be loved by someone who isn't thrown by their more sensitive reactions to the world, someone who can reassure and ground them in the security of a more realistic and enduring love. Being such an imaginative, thoughtful and spiritual person, Pisces' love needs to be met with understanding in order to help them feel secure. Forget 'treat them mean to keep them keen' as this will just alienate tender-hearted Pisces, whose ego can't be bothered with that sort of game playing. They are very much an all-or-nothing type.

Ultimately, as long as they remember to keep some sort of grip on reality and not let their heart rule their head completely, Pisces can be happy in love. They must remember not to use love as a manufactured opportunity for escapism from real life, however, but learn to recognise the 'real thing' which will last.

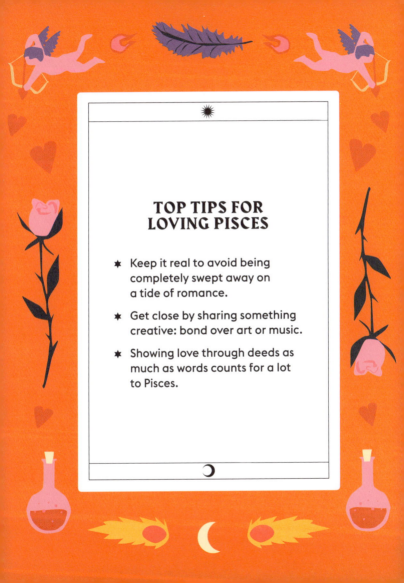

TOP TIPS FOR LOVING PISCES

★ Keep it real to avoid being completely swept away on a tide of romance.

★ Get close by sharing something creative: bond over art or music.

★ Showing love through deeds as much as words counts for a lot to Pisces.

Pisces' sex life

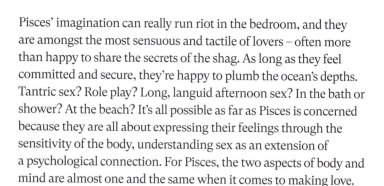

Pisces' imagination can really run riot in the bedroom, and they are amongst the most sensuous and tactile of lovers – often more than happy to share the secrets of the shag. As long as they feel committed and secure, they're happy to plumb the ocean's depths. Tantric sex? Role play? Long, languid afternoon sex? In the bath or shower? At the beach? It's all possible as far as Pisces is concerned because they are all about expressing their feelings through the sensitivity of the body, understanding sex as an extension of a psychological connection. For Pisces, the two aspects of body and mind are almost one and the same when it comes to making love.

There can be a playfulness, too, as Pisces is usually blessed with a youthful inclination, whatever their age. As long as they're not trying to bury any uncomfortable feelings or using sex as escapism, Pisces can be a light-hearted, fun lover as often as they are intense; a lover who likes to confer pleasure as much as receive it. In many ways, they can be one of the easiest and most liberated of lovers, but not for someone in a hurry. Sex with Pisces is usually an imaginative three-course meal, not a snack.

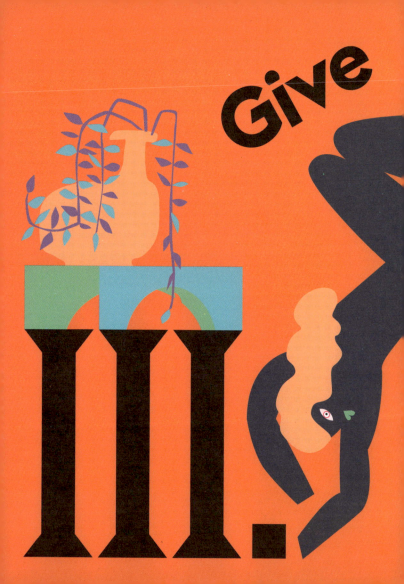

Give

III.

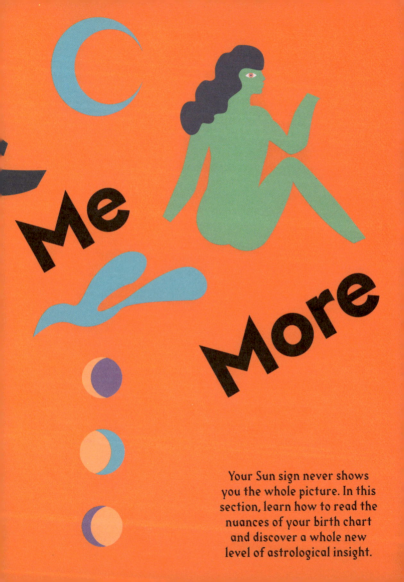

Me & More

Your Sun sign never shows you the whole picture. In this section, learn how to read the nuances of your birth chart and discover a whole new level of astrological insight.

Your birth chart

Your birth chart is a snapshot of a particular moment, in a particular place, at the precise moment of your birth and is therefore completely individual to you. It's like a blueprint, a map, a statement of occurrence, spelling out possible traits and influences – but it isn't your destiny. It is just a symbolic tool to which you can refer, based on the position of the planets at the time of your birth. If you can't get to an astrologer, these days anyone can get their birth chart prepared in minutes online (see page 108 for a list of websites and apps that will do it for you). Even if you don't know your exact time of birth, just knowing the date and place of birth can create the beginnings of a useful template.

Remember, nothing is intrinsically good or bad in astrology and there is no explicit timing or forecasting: it's more a question of influences and how these might play out positively or negatively. And if we have some insight, and some tools with which to approach, see or interpret our circumstances and surroundings, this gives us something to work with.

When you are reading your birth chart, it's useful to first understand the tools of astrology available to you; not only the astrological signs and what they represent, but also the 10 planets referred to in astrology and their individual characteristics, along with the 12 houses and what they mean. Individually, these tools of astrology are of passing interest, but when you start to see how they might sit in juxtaposition to each other, then the bigger picture becomes more accessible and we begin to gain insights that can be useful to us.

Broadly speaking, each of the planets suggests a different type of energy, the astrological signs propose the various ways in which that energy might be expressed, while the houses represent areas of experience in which this expression might operate.

Next to bring into the picture are the positions of the signs at four key points: the ascendant, or rising sign, and its opposite, the descendant; and the midheaven and its opposite, the IC, not to mention the different aspects created by congregations of signs and planets.

It is now possible to see how subtle the reading of a birth chart might be and how it is infinite in its variety, and highly specific to an individual. With this information, and a working understanding of the symbolic meaning and influences of the signs, planets and houses of your unique astrological profile, you can begin to use these tools to help with decision-making and other aspects of life.

Reading your chart

If you have your birth chart prepared, either by hand or via an online program, you will see a circle divided into 12 segments, with information clustered at various points indicating the position of each zodiac sign, in which segment it appears and at what degree. Irrespective of the features that are relevant to the individual, each chart follows the same pattern when it comes to interpretation.

Given the time of birth, the place of birth and the position of the planets at that moment, the birth chart, sometimes called a natal horoscope, is drawn up.

If you consider the chart as a clock face, the first house (see pages 95–99 for the astrological houses) begins at the 9, and it is from this point that, travelling anti-clockwise the chart is read from the first house, through the 12 segments of the chart to the twelfth.

The beginning point, the 9, is also the point at which the Sun rises on your life, giving you your ascendant, or rising sign, and opposite to this, at the 3 of the clock face, is your descendant sign. The midheaven point of your chart, the MC, is at 12, and its opposite, the IC, at 6 (see pages 101–102).

Understanding the significance of the characteristics of the astrological signs and the planets, their particular energies, their placements and their aspects to each other can be helpful in understanding ourselves and our relationships with others. In day-to-day life, too, the changing configuration of planets and their effects are much more easily understood with a basic knowledge of astrology, as are the recurring patterns that can sometimes strengthen and sometimes delay opportunities and possibilities. Working with, rather than against, these trends can make life more manageable and, in the last resort, more successful.

The Moon effect

If your Sun sign represents your consciousness, your life force and your individual will, then the Moon represents that side of your personality that you tend to keep rather secret or hidden. This is the realm of instinct, intuition, creativity and the unconscious, which can take you places emotionally that are sometimes hard to understand. This is what brings great subtlety and nuance to a person, way beyond just their Sun sign. So you may have your Sun in Pisces, and all that means, but this might be countered by a strongly practical and grounded Moon in Taurus; or you may have your Sun in open-hearted Leo, but a Moon in Aquarius with all its rebellious, emotional detachment.

Phases of the Moon

The Moon orbits the Earth, taking roughly 28 days to do so. How much of the Moon we see is determined by how much of the Sun's light it reflects, giving us the impression that it waxes, or grows, and wanes. When the Moon is new, to us, only a sliver of it is illuminated. As it waxes, it reflects more light and moves from a crescent, to a waxing crescent to a first quarter; then it moves to a waxing gibbous Moon, to a full Moon. Then the Moon begins to wane through a waning gibbous, to a last quarter, and then the cycle begins again. All of this occurs over four weeks. When we have two full Moons in any one calendar month, the second is called a blue Moon.

Each month the Moon also moves through an astrological sign, as we know from our personal birth charts. This, too, will yield information – a Moon in Scorpio can have a very different effect to one in Capricorn – and depending on our personal charts, this can have a shifting influence each month. For example, if the Moon in your birth chart is in Virgo, then when the actual Moon moves into Virgo, this will have an additional influence. Read the characteristics of the signs for further information (see pages 12–17).

The Moon's cycle has an energetic effect, which we can see quite easily on the ocean tides. Astrologically, because the Moon is both a fertility symbol and attuned to our deeper psychological side, we can use this to focus more profoundly and creatively on aspects of life that are important to us.

Eclipses

Generally speaking, an eclipse covers up and prevents light being shed on a situation. Astrologically speaking, this will depend on where the Sun or Moon is positioned in relation to other planets at the time of an eclipse. So if a solar eclipse is in Gemini, there will be a Geminian influence or an influence on Geminis.

Hiding, or shedding, light on an area of our lives is an invitation to pay attention to it. Eclipses are generally about beginnings or endings, which is why our ancestors saw them as portents, important signs to be taken notice of. As it is possible to know when an eclipse is forthcoming, these are charted astronomically; consequently, their astrological significance can be assessed and acted upon ahead of time.

The 10 planets

For the purpose of astrology (but not for astronomy, because the Sun is really a star) we talk about 10 planets, and each astrological sign has a ruling planet, with Mercury, Venus and Mars each being assigned two. The characteristics of each planet describe those influences that can affect signs, all of which information feeds into the interpretation of a birth chart.

The Moon

This sign is an opposing principle to the Sun, forming a pair, and it represents the feminine, symbolising containment and receptivity, how we react most instinctively and with feeling.

Rules the sign of Cancer.

The Sun

The Sun represents the masculine, and is seen as the energy that sparks life, which suggests a paternal energy in our birth chart. It also symbolises our self or essential being, and our purpose.

Rules the sign of Leo.

Mercury

Mercury is the planet of communication and symbolises our urge to make sense of, understand and communicate our thoughts through words.

Rules the signs of Gemini and Virgo.

Venus

The planet of love is all about attraction, connection and pleasure and in a female chart it symbolises her style of femininity, while in a male chart it represents his ideal partner.

Rules the signs of Taurus and Libra.

Mars

This planet symbolises pure energy (Mars was, after all, the god of War) but it also tells you in which areas you're most likely to be assertive, aggressive or to take risks.

Rules the signs of Aries and Scorpio.

Saturn

Saturn is sometimes called the wise teacher or taskmaster of astrology, symbolising lessons learnt and limitations, showing us the value of determination, tenacity and resilience.

Rules the sign of Capricorn.

Jupiter

The planet Jupiter is the largest in our solar system and symbolises bounty and benevolence, all that is expansive and jovial. Like the sign it rules, it's also about moving away from the home on journeys and exploration.

Rules the sign of Sagittarius.

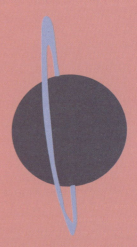

Uranus

This planet symbolises the unexpected, new ideas and innovation, and the urge to tear down the old and usher in the new. The downside can mark an inability to fit in and consequently the feeling of being an outsider.

Rules the sign of Aquarius.

Pluto

Aligned to Hades (*Pluto* in Latin), the god of the underworld or death, this planet exerts a powerful force that lies below the surface and which, in its most negative form, can represent obsessions and compulsive behaviour.

Rules the sign of Scorpio.

Neptune

Linked to the sea, this is about what lies beneath, underwater and too deep to be seen clearly. Sensitive, intuitive and artistic, it also symbolises the capacity to love unconditionally, to forgive and forget.

Rules the sign of Pisces.

The four elements

Further divisions of the 12 astrological signs into the four elements of earth, fire, air and water yield other characteristics. This comes from ancient Greek medicine, where the body was considered to be made up of four bodily fluids or 'humours'. These four humours – blood, yellow bile, black bile and phlegm – corresponded to the four temperaments of sanguine, choleric, melancholic and phlegmatic, to the four seasons of the year, spring, summer, autumn, winter, and the four elements of air, fire, earth and water.

Related to astrology, these symbolic qualities cast further light on characteristics of the different signs. Carl Jung also used them in his psychology, and we still refer to people as earthy, fiery, airy or wet in their approach to life, while sometimes describing people as 'being in their element'. In astrology, those Sun signs that share the same element are said to have an affinity, or an understanding, with each other.

Like all aspects of astrology, there is always a positive and a negative, and a knowledge of any 'shadow side' can be helpful in terms of self-knowledge and what we may need to enhance or balance out, particularly in our dealings with others.

Air

GEMINI ✳ LIBRA ✳ AQUARIUS

The realm of ideas is where these air signs excel. Perceptive and visionary and able to see the big picture, there is a very reflective quality to air signs that helps to vent situations. Too much air, however, can dissipate intentions, so Gemini might be indecisive, Libra has a tendency to sit on the fence, while Aquarius can be very disengaged.

Fire

ARIES ✳ LEO ✳ SAGITTARIUS

There is a warmth and energy to these signs, a positive approach, spontaneity and enthusiasm that can be inspiring and very motivational to others. The downside is that Aries has a tendency to rush in headfirst, Leo can have a need for attention and Sagittarius can tend to talk it up but not deliver.

Earth

TAURUS ✸ VIRGO ✸ CAPRICORN

Characteristically, these signs enjoy sensual pleasure, relishing food and other physical satisfactions, and they like to feel grounded, preferring to base their ideas in facts. The downside is that Taureans can be stubborn, Virgos can be pernickety and Capricorns can veer towards a dogged conservatism.

Water

CANCER ✸ SCORPIO ✸ PISCES

Water signs are very responsive, like the tide ebbing and flowing, and can be very perceptive and intuitive, sometimes uncannily so because of their ability to feel. The downside is – watery enough – a tendency to feel swamped, and then Cancer can be both tenacious and self-protective, Pisces chameleon-like in their attention and Scorpio unpredictable and intense.

Cardinal, fixed and mutable signs

In addition to the 12 signs being divided into four elements, they can also be grouped into three different ways in which their energies may act or react, giving further depth to each sign's particular characteristics.

Cardinal

ARIES * CANCER * LIBRA * CAPRICORN

These are action planets, with an energy that takes the initiative and gets things started. Aries has the vision, Cancer the feelings, Libra the contacts and Capricorn the strategy.

Fixed

TAURUS ✳ LEO ✳ SCORPIO ✳ AQUARIUS

Slower but more determined, these signs work to progress and maintain those initiatives that the cardinal signs have fired up. Taurus offers physical comfort, Leo loyalty, Scorpio emotional support and Aquarius sound advice. You can count on fixed signs, but they tend to resist change.

Mutable

GEMINI ✳ VIRGO ✳ SAGITTARIUS ✳ PISCES

Adaptable and responsive to new ideas, places and people, mutable signs have a unique ability to adjust to their surroundings. Gemini is mentally agile, Virgo is practical and versatile, Sagittarius visualises possibilities and Pisces is responsive to change.

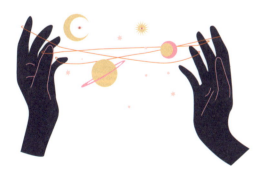

The 12 houses

The birth chart is divided into 12 houses, which represent separate areas and functions of your life. When you are told you have something in a specific house – for example, Libra (balance) in the fifth house (creativity and sex) – it creates a way of interpreting the influences that can arise and are particular to how you might approach an aspect of your life.

Each house relates to a Sun sign, and in this way each is represented by some of the characteristics of that sign, which is said to be its natural ruler.

Three of these houses are considered to be mystical, relating to our interior, psychic world: the fourth (home), eighth (death and regeneration) and twelfth (secrets).

1st House

THE SELF

RULED BY ARIES

This house symbolises the self: you, who you are and how you represent yourself, your likes, dislikes and approach to life. It also represents how you see yourself and what you want in life.

2nd House

POSSESSIONS

RULED BY TAURUS

The second house symbolises your possessions, what you own, including money; how you earn or acquire your income; and your material security and the physical things you take with you as you move through life.

3rd House

COMMUNICATION

RULED BY GEMINI

This house is about communication and mental attitude, primarily how you express yourself. It's also about how you function within your family, and how you travel to school or work, and includes how you think, speak, write and learn.

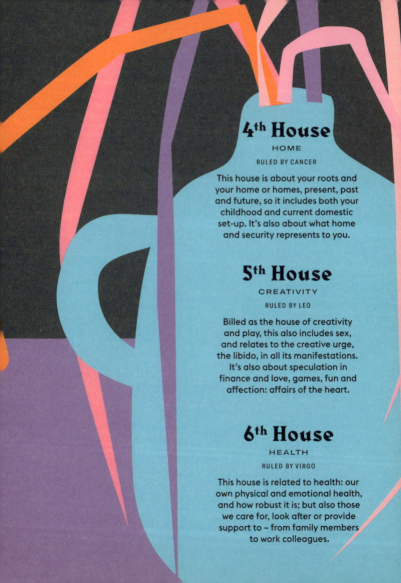

4th House

HOME

RULED BY CANCER

This house is about your roots and your home or homes, present, past and future, so it includes both your childhood and current domestic set-up. It's also about what home and security represents to you.

5th House

CREATIVITY

RULED BY LEO

Billed as the house of creativity and play, this also includes sex, and relates to the creative urge, the libido, in all its manifestations. It's also about speculation in finance and love, games, fun and affection: affairs of the heart.

6th House

HEALTH

RULED BY VIRGO

This house is related to health: our own physical and emotional health, and how robust it is; but also those we care for, look after or provide support to – from family members to work colleagues.

7th House

PARTNERSHIPS

RULED BY LIBRA

The opposite of the first house, this reflects shared goals and intimate partnerships, our choice of life partner and how successful our relationships might be. It also reflects partnerships and adversaries in our professional world.

8th House

REGENERATION

RULED BY SCORPIO

For death, read regeneration or spiritual transformation: this house also reflects legacies and what you inherit after death, in personality traits or materially. And because regeneration requires sex, it's also about sex and sexual emotions.

9th House

TRAVEL

RULED BY SAGITTARIUS

The house of long-distance travel and exploration, this is also about the broadening of the mind that travel can bring, and how that might express itself. It also reflects the sending out of ideas, which can come about from literary effort or publication.

11th House

FRIENDSHIPS

RULED BY AQUARIUS

The eleventh house is about friendship groups and acquaintances, vision and ideas, and is less about immediate gratification but more concerning longer-term dreams and how these might be realised through our ability to work harmoniously with others.

12th House

SECRETS

RULED BY PISCES

Considered the most spiritual house, it is also the house of the unconscious, of secrets and of what might lie hidden, the metaphorical skeleton in the closet. It also reflects the secret ways we might self-sabotage or imprison our own efforts by not exploring them.

10th House

ASPIRATIONS

RULED BY CAPRICORN

This represents our aspiration and status, how we'd like to be elevated in public standing (or not), our ambitions, image and what we'd like to attain in life, through our own efforts.

The ascendant

Otherwise known as your rising sign, this is the sign of the zodiac that appears at the horizon as dawn breaks on the day of your birth, depending on your location in the world and time of birth. This is why knowing your time of birth is a useful factor in astrology, because your 'rising sign' yields a lot of information about those aspects of your character that are more on show, how you present yourself and how you are seen by others. So, even if you are a Sun Pisces, but have Cancer rising, you may be seen as someone who is maternal, with a noticeable commitment to the domestic life in one way or another. Knowing your own ascendant – or that of another person – will often help explain why there doesn't seem to be such a direct correlation between their personality and their Sun sign.

As long as you know your time of birth and where you were born, working out your ascendant using an online tool or app is very easy (see page 108). Just ask your mum or other family members, or check your birth certificate (in those countries that include a birth time). If the astrological chart were a clock face, the ascendant is at the 9 o'clock position.

The descendant

The descendant gives an indication of a possible life partner, based on the idea that opposites attract. Once you know your ascendant, the descendant is easy to work out as it is always six signs away: for example, if your ascendant is Virgo, your descendant is Pisces. If the astrological chart were a clock face, the descendant would be at the 3 o'clock position.

The midheaven (MC)

Also included in the birth chart is the position of the midheaven or MC (from the Latin, *medium coeli*, meaning middle of the heavens), which indicates your attitude towards your work, career and professional standing. If the astrological chart were a clock face, the MC would be at the 12 o'clock position.

The IC

Finally, your IC (from the Latin, *imum coeli*, meaning the lowest part of the heavens) indicates your attitude towards your home and family, and is also related to the end of your life. Your IC will be six signs away from your MC: for example, if your MC is Aquarius, your IC is Leo. If the astrological chart were a clock face, the IC is at the 6 o'clock position.

Saturn return

Saturn is one of the slower-moving planets, taking around 28 years to complete its orbit around the Sun and return to the place it occupied at the time of your birth. This return can last between two to three years and be very noticeable in the period coming up to our thirtieth and sixtieth birthdays, often considered to be significant 'milestone' birthdays.

Because the energy of Saturn is sometimes experienced as demanding, this isn't always an easy period of life. A wise teacher or a hard taskmaster, some consider the Saturn effect as 'cruel to be kind' in the way that many good teachers can be, keeping us on track like a rigorous personal trainer.

Everyone experiences their Saturn return relevant to their circumstances, but it is a good time to take stock, let go of the stuff in your life that no longer serves you, revise your expectations while being unapologetic about what you would like to include more of in your life. So if you are experiencing or anticipating this life event, embrace and work with it because what you learn now – about yourself, mainly – is worth knowing, however turbulent it might be, and can pay dividends in how you manage the next 28 years!

Mercury retrograde

Even those with little interest in astrology often take notice when the planet Mercury is retrograde. Astrologically, retrogrades are periods when planets are stationary but, as we continue to move forwards, Mercury 'appears' to move backwards. There is a shadow period either side of a retrograde period, when it could be said to be slowing down or speeding up, which can also be a little turbulent. Generally speaking, the advice is not to make any important moves related to communication on a retrograde and, even if a decision is made, know that it's likely to change.

Given that Mercury is the planet of communication, you can immediately see why there are concerns about its retrograde status and its link to communication failures – of the old-fashioned sort when the post office loses a letter, or the more modern technological variety when your computer crashes

– causing problems. Mercury retrograde can also affect travel, with delays in flights or train times, traffic jams or collisions. Mercury also influences personal communications: listening, speaking, being heard (or not), and can cause confusion or arguments. It can also affect more formal agreements, like contracts between buyer and seller.

These retrograde periods occur three to four times a year, lasting for roughly three weeks, with a shadow period either side. The dates in which it happens also means it occurs within a specific astrological sign. If, for example, it occurs between 25 October and 15 November, its effect would be linked to the characteristics of Scorpio. In addition, those Sun sign Scorpios, or those with Scorpio in significant placements in their chart, may also experience a greater effect.

Mercury retrograde dates are easy to find from an astrological table, or ephemeris, and online. These can be used in order to avoid planning events that might be affected around these times. How Mercury retrograde may affect you more personally requires knowledge of your birth chart and an understanding of its more specific combination of influences with the signs and planets in your chart.

If you are going to weather a Mercury retrograde more easily, be aware that glitches can occur so, to some extent, expect delays and double-check details. Stay positive if postponements occur and consider this period an opportunity to slow down, review or reconsider ideas in your business or your personal life. Use the time to correct mistakes or reshape plans, preparing for when any stuck energy can shift and you can move forward again more smoothly.

Further reading

Astrology Decoded (2013)
by Sue Merlyn Farebrother;
published by Rider

Astrology for Dummies
(2007) by Rae Orion;
published by Wiley Publishing

*Chart Interpretation
Handbook: Guidelines for
Understanding the Essentials
of the Birth Chart* (1990)
by Stephen Arroyo;
published by CRCS
Publications

Jung's Studies in Astrology
(2018) by Liz Greene;
published by RKP

*The Only Astrology
Book You'll Ever Need*
(2012) by Joanne Woolfolk;
published by Taylor Trade

Websites

astro.com

astrologyzone.com

jessicaadams.com

shelleyvonstrunkel.com

Apps

Astrostyle

Co-Star

Susan Miller's Astrology Zone

The Daily Horoscope

The Pattern

Time Passages

Acknowledgements

Particular thanks are due to my trusty
team of Taureans. Firstly, to Kate Pollard,
Publishing Director at Hardie Grant, for her
passion for beautiful books and for commissioning
this series. And to Bex Fitzsimons for all her good
natured and conscientious editing. And finally to
Evi O. Studio, whose illustration and design talents
have produced small works of art. With such a
star-studded team, these books can only
shine and for that, my thanks.

About the author

Stella Andromeda has been studying astrology for over 30 years, believing that a knowledge of the constellations of the skies and their potential for psychological interpretation can be a useful tool. This extension of her study into book form makes modern insights about the ancient wisdom of the stars easily accessible, sharing her passion that reflection and self-knowledge only empowers us in life. With her sun in Taurus, Aquarius ascendant and moon in Cancer, she utilises earth, air and water to inspire her own astrological journey.

Published in 2019 by Hardie Grant Books,
an imprint of Hardie Grant Publishing

Hardie Grant Books (London)
5th & 6th Floors
52–54 Southwark Street
London, SE1 1UN

Hardie Grant Books (Melbourne)
Building 1, 658 Church Street
Richmond, Victoria 3121

hardiegrantbooks.com

British Library Cataloguing-in-Publication Data. A catalogue record
for this book is available from the British Library.

Pisces
ISBN: 9781784882686
10 9 8 7 6 5 4

Publishing Director: Kate Pollard
Junior Editor: Bex Fitzsimons
Art Direction and Illustrations: Evi O. Studio
Editor: Wendy Hobson
Production Controller: Sinead Hering

Colour reproduction by p2d
Printed and bound in China by Leo Paper Products Ltd.